ENNEAGRAM 3

Paths to Wholeness

by

Éilís Bergin PBVM and Eddie Fitzgerald SDB

Dedication

For Mary Cheyrou-Lagréze,
our many friends in Paris,
and those who attended our first
Enneagram Presenter's Course.
· Flyers all.

Cover Art: © Volk.

Designed, published and distributed by:
SDB MEDIA, Salesian College, Celbridge, Co. Kildare
Tel: (01) 627 5060
Fax: (01) 630 3601
E-mail: sdbmedia@eircom.net
Web: http://homepage.eircom.net/~sdbmedia

CHANGING THE TAPE

Sometimes when you work with sophisticated modern equipment things go wrong - often at the most inconvenient moment.

Whenever that happens to us, we like to recall the story of the rather nervous passenger travelling by air from Dublin to New York. An hour into the flight, when he's had time to calm down and begun to relax, he hears a voice over the intercom saying:

"This is your Captain speaking. We're happy to have you on board today. Our flying time to New York is seven and a half hours. We should arrive there at 14.30 hours local time. We're now travelling at a height of 30,000 feet and our cruising speed is 500 miles per hour. We've just switched on the automatic pilot and nothing can go wrong...go wrong...go wrong..."

AUTOMATIC PILOT

The fact is that the vast majority of us go through life on automatic pilot. We protect ourselves in so many ways from the reality around us, that we've convinced ourselves *that's* all the reality there is. We live in a trance, responding to people and events in patterned and relatively predictable ways.

We began this process very early in life. According to Enneagram theory there is a real distinction to be made between *essence* and *personality*. Our essence is who we really are, the self we experience when we journey to our innermost being. This self is gifted with a wide range of values, faculties and abilities to help us deal with the world in which we find ourselves.

Our particular temperament inclines us to favour some of these values and abilities more than others. Though we are capable of realizing them all, we tend to favour and develop our preferred ways of thinking, feeling and doing. This is not a problem so long as we remain open and flexible to adopting other ways of doing things when the need arises.

The difficulty is that we need ideal conditions (parenting, environment, schooling etc.) to become who we really are, and these conditions are not always available. The world we live in can be a very threatening and dangerous place. When we experience our world as somehow hostile, we learn very quickly how vulnerable and fragile we are. In order to protect our true self, we attempt to cover it up with our personality - the public face of the private self. In this way we hope to minimize the threats, make ourselves attractive and ensure that we are secure. Effectively, we do what we have to, in order to be respected, cared for and loved.

The down-side is that in doing so, we inevitably distort the values we've been blessed with, and overidentify with an idealized self-image which is no more than a partial expression of who we really are. The result is that we become locked into narrower and more rigid ways of thinking and less able to access the wide variety of appropriate strengths and abilities available to us.

When we become psychologically unhealthy this can lead to tunnel vision, which means we tend to see reality from one perspective only. By then we have lost contact with our centre and find our problem-solving resources limited to predictable, patterned and automatic responses.

THE POWER TO CHANGE

The great strength of the Enneagram is that it makes us aware of the unconscious patterns which so frequently rule and ruin our lives. It is a study of inscapes, not landscapes. In effect, it reveals our hidden map of reality - the core beliefs and assumptions which radically shape our personality. While it is true that the map is not the territory, this is already a giant step in the direction of positive change and personal development. It allows us once again to access and actualize our core strengths, so that gradually we can become who we truly are once more.

We do this by a process of *waking up* and *letting go*. We wake up to the real motivating energy which drives us to think, say and do things, and then gradually begin the process of letting go of our compulsiveness by accessing the strengths and avoiding the weaknesses of all the other types. This process of becoming a well-rounded, whole human being is continuous throughout life. There is no arrival point where we can finally say "I have it made!" - at least not this side of the grave. The reality is that when we think we 'have it made' we are back in our entranced state and in big trouble. We've switched on our automatic pilot once more, and cruise along as if nothing can go wrong...go wrong...go wrong.

Fortunately, understanding and working with the *Subtypes, Wings* and *Arrows* helps jog us out of our complacency and allows us to get in touch with our essence once more.

SUBTYPES

The Enneagram is a sophisticated model of how different personalities function. It argues that there are nine basic personality types, each with its own significantly different motivating energy or compulsion. However, each type is further divided into three subtypes which have their roots in our most basic survival instincts: *self-preservation* (our personal survival), *sexual* (how we survive and relate in one-to-one situations), and *social* (how we survive and relate in groups, in community or in society).

Over time, one of these subtypes became our preferred way of focusing on survival issues, dominating the other two. Another takes on secondary importance, while the third is often neglected. This means, for example, that someone who is a sexual subtype tends to act out of that energy focus, unless faced with serious self-survival or social-survival issues. An oversimplified example is when people are preparing to go on holidays. Some people (*self-preservation*) will be preoccupied with making sure they have everything they need to avoid disaster, bringing with them the proverbial 'kitchen sink'. Others (*sexual*) will be more concerned with ensuring that they have a stimulating companion for the duration. Finally, there are those (*social*) who are more excited about the interesting people they will meet or stay with during their break.

The less we know about what makes us tick, the more likely we are to be manipulated by it. Therefore, discovering our preferred subtype enables us to grow in self-awareness and allows us to home in on our exaggerated and inflexible preoccupations and patterns of response. This can help highlight our strengths and weaknesses, enable us to take more charge of our choice, and bring balance to the way we deal with the different situations in which we find ourselves.

The subtypes are also very helpful in distinguishing between people of the same type. Since subtype behaviour frequently predominates over the more general type responses, subtypes give a nuance to the personality types and make it possible for us to distinguish a total of 27 different personality styles,

Distinguishing Subtypes

In this booklet we outline the main concerns of the subtypes for each of the nine Enneagram personality styles. We suggest you read through the subtypes which relate to your own personality type and see which one is nearest to your preferred survival mechanism. It's worth noting in general that:

(a) *Self-preservation subtypes are concerned with personal, day-to-day survival.* They are usually defensive, cautious, self-sufficient and private. Their preoccupation is with having enough resources to meet any unforeseen demand or crisis.

(b) *Sexual subtypes are concerned with intimate or one-to-one relationships.* They are generally energized, competitive and intense. Their preoccupation is to be loved or at least paid attention to by one significant other.

(c) *Social subtypes are concerned with group or community relationships.* They generally enjoy being with people and are stimulated by them. Social justice issues make them feel part of a larger whole.

The path to wholeness lies in balance and harmony. When we find our preferred subtype we are in a better position to move towards integration of all our survival mechanisms and break free of the more compulsive and destructive elements of our basic personality style.

WINGS

In Enneagram terms, the *Wings* are the personality types on either side of our own type. Thus, the Wings for the Observer (Five) are the Artist (Four) and the Supporter (Six). The Wings nuance our personality type even further. For example, a Five with a Six Wing may be suspicious and anxious, while a Five with a Four Wing may be more emotional and flamboyant. As with the Subtypes, we have here another way of differentiating the nine basic types.

In our own workshops and interviews we have found that the theory of each type having two Wings fits in with most people's experience. What appears to happen is that, even when we are still young, we begin to realize that our basic personality style can become so distorted that it needs some help to minimize its worst excesses. This leads us to rely on the Wing type that is likeliest to help us in our dealings with those around us. It is only later on in our growth process that we become aware that our other Wing can also assist us.

In Ireland when people want to offer a friend a second drink, they rationalize it by saying that "a bird never flew on one wing." We believe the phrase makes good sense in Enneagram terms. The insight of Wing theory (and, indeed, that of the Arrows), is that any energy which enables us to break free of our patterned and distorted outlook on life is a positive step in waking us up from our entranced, compulsive view of the world.

The central dynamic of the Enneagram is to reveal to us our partial view of reality and to encourage us to open our eyes to the broader picture by accessing the strengths and avoiding the weaknesses of all the other types.

The measure in which we succeed in incorporating the virtues of the other eight personality styles is the measure in which we become whole human beings.

It is only fair to add that some Enneagram teachers prefer to speak about having only one Wing, while a minority argue that the whole theory is a non-starter.

ARROWS

When we're stressed we think and feel differently from when we're secure. According to Enneagram theory, what happens is that we take on the characteristics of the personality type at our *stress point*, which is the type the Arrow points *towards*. Similarly, when we are relaxed we tend to adopt the characteristics of the personality type at our *security point*, the type the Arrow points *away from*.

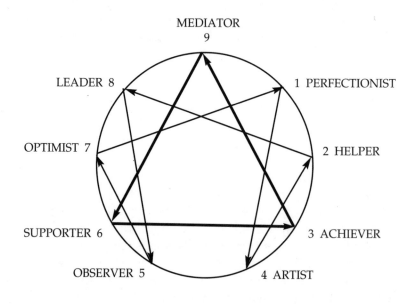

ARROWS AND PERSONALITY TYPES

Even though at times it may look like it, we never become a different personality type. However, our stress and security points do influence us both positively and negatively. The secret is to be aware that this is happening and so be able to take steps to emphasize the positive and eliminate the negative, as appropriate.

Plus and Minus
When our backs are against the wall, the vast majority of us generally revert to type. We go back to what we know best - our customary patterns of behaviour. When things go wrong, our immediate reaction is not to look for new options, but simply to overplay the game we're already playing. We are like fanatics, who redouble their efforts while losing sight of their aim. Or like the impatient driver who, when his wife tells him they're lost, immediately replies: "Forget it. We're making great time!"

Interestingly, while most people consider stress to be a negative condition and security a positive one, this is not always true. Stress can often bring out the very best in us, and be a very positive experience, while security can lull us into a false and egotistical sense of our own importance, thus preventing us from developing to our full potential.

This is why we have included both plus (+) and minus (-) elements for the Arrow influences on each personality type. When stressed, we generally follow the line of least resistance and tend to pick up the negative characteristics of the appropriate type. But we can always 'change the tape' and access the more positive qualities. This is an essential part of growth. The opposite is true for our security point: it is basically a positive source of energy, but can also include many negative elements.

It is helpful to remember that we can find the positive in everything - if we know where to look. It's also important to understand that we all experience stress and security differently - one person's meat is another's poison. So the emotional and mental shift which takes place within us comes about mainly when our individual stress and security levels are high and enduring.

11

By familiarizing ourselves with what may happen with our type when experiencing prolonged and high-level stress or security, we will be in a better position to access the more positive elements and avoid the negative. In this way we will be taking charge of our choice. Most of us sleepwalk our way through life. Waking up to what's really happening is the beginning of wisdom.

TAKING FLIGHT

We began with a story about flying. Here's another, this time from the philosopher-theologian Kierkegaard. He talked about a group of geese, who waddled around their farmyard all day long. They were very comfortable, well fed and had a good deal of space to pace about. But it was all quite boring and uninspiring. Until, that is, one day they encountered a stranger in their midst. He seemed to be a preaching goose, because he spoke at length about their forefathers and how they had journeyed across the trackless wastes of the sky and travelled vast distances to experience other lands. The farmyard geese could feel the tingle of excitement in their blood, and longings they couldn't explain moved them to the core. Their horizons were expanded as they heard about their ancestors, and they applauded the preaching goose, sharing their corn and barn with him. All this they did. But one thing they never did. They did not fly.

It's sad that so many people are content to remain at the level represented by the farmyard geese. When we are reasonably well fed, clothed, housed and cared for, we seem quite satisfied and content. But the longings are there and the reality is that we are settling for less. The Enneagram shows us what we truly desire and gives us strategies for obtaining it. It is our earnest hope that those who come across this booklet will be open to letting go of the predictable and patterned responses which hold them down, and truly learn to fly.

ONES

If you have adopted this personality style you are gifted in many ways. In particular, you are:

- idealistic
- diligent
- fair
- principled
- honest
- dependable
- orderly
- conscientious
- ethical

However, like everyone else, you have your flaws. For example, you can be:

- uptight
- judgemental
- moralistic
- critical
- inflexible
- puritanical
- impatient
- controlling
- dogmatic

As a **Perfectionist** you strive so hard to make everything and everyone as good as possible that you have become deeply angry at any imperfection But you are so oblivious of your *anger* that you deny how controlling and destructive it is.

SUBTYPES

Self-Preservation: *Focus on Anxiety*
For you life is more of a struggle than a gift. You believe love has to be earned and are convinced that you get what you pay for. To survive you are convinced you have to hold on to what you have, and be prepared for every eventuality - "what's mine is my own - I earned it." Therefore, to be dependent is threatening for your essentially go-it-alone mentality.

Your anger is transformed into anxiety or relentless worrying. This is manifested in survival issues like having everything you need in all circumstances, getting things precisely right, planning future events, dealing with personal problems etc. You possess a built-in radar to reveal hidden threats, slights or injustices, and direct your special resentment at those who apparently float through life without a care. Interestingly, this may reveal your own hidden needs.

Sexual: *Focus on Jealousy*
Your idealization of one-to-one relationship leads to a certain possessiveness. It can also result in an anxiety that others will be considered more desirable because more caring, clever, attractive or fun than yourself.

Your anger appears as a jealous vigilance which keeps your antennae ever active, scanning for any imagined coolness or rejection. The build-up of resentment within you and the continual comparison with others makes for occasional heated exchanges or outbursts. Generally though it simply festers.

The pain of constant comparison of yourself with others is channelled into jealousy at another's success, popularity, job promotion, social skills etc. Because enjoyment has to be earned, you see any perceived threat to it as unfair or potentially disastrous.

Social: *Focus on (Non-)Adaptability*
Involvement in correct causes (political, social, religious) is vital to you. There is one right viewpoint - yours. When your convictions clash with others you find it hard to be flexible, especially when you think the right, the good and the true are at stake.

Your anger generally comes out as frustration or criticism of yourself or the group for not being perfect. You are unwilling or even unable to compromise, to give and take, to make allowances or to tolerate less worthy motives than the best. When convinced of a course of action it is hard for you to keep an open mind or appreciate alternative positions. Where groups fail to measure up to set standards you find yourself constantly sniping at them. You may attempt to improve the group or, failing that, take the high moral ground and leave.

WINGS 9 & 2

As you grew up you began to realize that your dogged persistence, as well as your pickiness, attention to detail and generally critical and preachy approach were a turn-off. After all, most people prefer to be praised rather than blamed, and to meet people who accept them as they are, faults and all. So you began to rely on the personality style nearest to you to give your own style some balance. You may, for example, have spotted that *impatience* is among the list of your characteristic flaws. But *patience* is one of the strengths of your Nine Wing. When you learn to incorporate your wing-strength into your own personality style, you begin to soar.

Nine Wing: When you access the strengths of your Nine Wing you have a gut combination. The Nine influence allows you to remain responsible but in a much more relaxed fashion. It also means you will be inclined to seek harmony rather than constantly find fault, and that you will be able to 'hang loose' more. Additionally, you will be able to tolerate a greater amount of untidiness in your life. There is a danger, though, that you will procrastinate even more than usual.

Two Wing: When you access the strengths of your Two Wing you have a gut/heart combination. This will help you in a different way. With it you become more altruistic and concerned for others. This means that you will be better able to deal in a more balanced way with both tasks and people. It also means you will be less likely to burn out, because you are learning to use both intuition and feelings to deal with issues satisfactorily. You will, however, need to be careful that you pay attention to your own needs, because Two energy is notoriously inclined to pay more attention to others' needs than its own.

Proper balance is achieved by accessing the strengths of

both your wings and taking care to avoid their characteristic weaknesses. When you do so, you learn to let go of your narrow Perfectionist viewpoint and begin to experience the advantages of other points of view.

ARROWS 4 & 7

The 'Arrow Theory' of the Enneagram can be very helpful when you are feeling either stressed or secure.

As a Perfectionist you are motivated by your need to be right, and become stressed when you say 'yes' too quickly, don't delegate, and things don't match your unrealistic expectations.

Almost as soon as the pressure begins to build up, you gradually tend to slide to the lower end of your own personality style. When this happens your natural tendency is to redouble your efforts, to try harder, to burn the midnight oil, and to push yourself to breaking point. All this feeds into your sense that life is unfair and that you are being hard done by. Sometimes, without even noticing it, you can spiral downward into anger and depression.

As your stress increases you find yourself all too easily adopting the *negative* characteristics of your Four stress point. However, this need not be an inevitable progression. You can, instead, get in touch with the *positive* side.

Four: (Stress Point)
- You re-direct your anger inside, fostering depression.
- You envy other people's ease and grace.
- You feel resentful that expectations are not being met.
- You lose self-confidence and feel unworthy of love.

+ *You develop your creative and artistic side.*
+ *You touch into your deepest feelings.*

When you are secure you are generally more in touch with the higher side of your personality style. As a One this

allows you to accept yourself much more, to be more tolerant of mistakes (your own and those of others), to let
things be rather than continually seek to change them.
This means you become much more compassionate and
forgiving, are better able to hold good and bad in balance
and less likely to insist on unrealistically high standards.

All of this feeds into the *positive* strengths of your Seven
security point. But, here too there can be some *negatives*.
Dealing with the pluses and minuses helps us grow.

Seven: (Security Point)

+ *You brighten up and begin to enjoy life.*
+ *You let go of rigidities and become more spontaneous.*
+ *You concentrate on the positive rather than negative.*
+ *You become more self-accepting and less judgmental.*

- You open the door to hidden excessive behaviours.
- You over-indulge in food, drink, sex, etc.

HELPFUL COPING CUES

❏ Relax and enjoy the moment.

❏ Lower your ceiling!

❏ When you can't cope, simplify.

❏ God can write straight with crooked lines.

❏ There's no such thing as instant growth.

❏ *Forgive and you will be forgiven. (Lk 6:37)*

TWOS

If you have adopted this personality style you are gifted in many ways. In particular, you are:

- □ caring
- □ sympathetic
- □ helpful
- □ considerate
- □ supportive
- □ adaptable
- □ generous
- □ self-sacrificing
- □ loving

However, like everyone else, you have your flaws. For example, you can be:

- □ dependent
- □ flattering
- □ hysterical
- □ needy
- □ interfering
- □ seductive
- □ possessive
- □ manipulative
- □ self-important

As a **Helper** you strive so hard to attend to other people's needs that you neglect your own and even pride yourself in having none. But you are so oblivious of your *pride* that you deny how controlling and destructive it is.

SUBTYPES

Self-Preservation: *Focus on Privilege*
You take pride in helping people and think of yourself as independent. You are frequently ashamed to ask for help. Your pride prevents you from doing so, unless it is a life-or-death issue. You feel insecure when left out. Selfless feelings cover up or suppress your own need for approval and protection.

Your desire for privilege is unmasked when others don't respond in kind. You indirectly work for yourself through working for others. This minimizes the pressures of personal competition and avoids possible failure or humiliation in public. When you help others succeed, *you* succeed and expect at least some preferential treatment (e.g. recognition for services rendered, introductions to dignataries or the best seats at the theatre). Effectively you are saying: "you scratch my back, and I'll scratch yours."

Sexual: *Focus on Seduction*
You tend to seduce others by supporting and adopting their interests, tastes and concerns. This makes you very attractive as a partner. You take pride in making others feel they are friends or lovers. This you do by turning on the charm, hanging on people's every word and dressing the part.

You are a pleaser, confidant, trusted companion and 'best friend' who makes others feel good and special. You are not afraid to pursue loved ones or business associates, and readily deal with hitches and problems in relationships. You choose who to go after, and keep going until you have snared him or her. This seduction and pursuit applies equally whether you are a man or a woman. Interestingly, you frequently choose those who are unavailable so as not to have to face your own hidden fear of intimacy. It's all in the chase!

Social: *Focus on Ambition*
Because you are socially ambitious, what counts is who you know and where you're seen. You take pride in your accomplishments, reputation, professional qualifications, public image and social standing. You like to back winners and are attracted to high achievers. Wanting to be part of the inner circle, you attach yourself to prominent figures (e.g. a financial guru, business leader or local dignitary), and achieve your ambitions on their coat-tails by being the indispensable power behind the throne.

You quickly learn to play the system and cut your cloth to the prevailing wind. You are sensitive to the slightest changes in mood and adapt accordingly to keep your rightful place. You lap up compliments, especially when these involve your indispensability. But you resent it when you are taken for granted.

WINGS 1 & 3

As you grew up you began to realize that your general unwillingness to receive, as well as your ability to make others feel guilty and your martyr complex, were a turn-off. After all, most people prefer to give and take, and to be permitted to help occasionally instead of having to receive all the time. So you began to rely on the personality style nearest to you to give your own style some balance. You may, for example, have spotted that *flattery* is among the list of your characteristic flaws. But *honesty* is one of the strengths of your One Wing. When you learn to incorporate your wing-strength into your own personality style, you begin to soar.

One Wing: When you access the strengths of your One Wing you have a heart/gut combination. The One influence allows you to give compliments honestly and not to be afraid to voice your reservations. It also ensures that you will stand up for your own rights more. Additionally, you will be more inclined to say and do things because they are right, rather than because they are helpful or the kind thing to do. There is a danger, though, that you will become overly critical of yourself and others, and over-responsible to the point of breakdown.

Three Wing: When you access the strengths of your Three Wing you have a heart combination. This will help you in a different way. With it you become more self-assured and independent. This means you will be more successful in handling intimate personal relationships and better able to facilitate groups. A whole social dimension is added to your normal perspective. You will, however, need to be careful of becoming more task orientated and image conscious, especially to please a boss or significant other.

Proper balance is achieved by accessing the strengths of *both* your wings and taking care to avoid their characteristic weaknesses. When you do so, you learn to let go of your obsessive Helper viewpoint and begin to experience the advantages of other points of view.

ARROWS 8 & 4

The 'Arrow Theory' of the Enneagram can be very helpful when you are feeling either stressed or secure.

As a Helper you are motivated by your need to be needed and loved, and become stressed by your difficulty in saying 'no', and by having to reveal your own needs and let others take care of you.

Almost as soon as the pressure begins to build up, you gradually tend to slide to the lower end of your own personality style. When this happens your natural tendency is to invest even more heavily in helping others to the point where you become a martyr to their cause. This can make you feel that others don't appreciate what you are doing for them and that they are victimizing you in some way. You can then become resentful, aggrieved, reproachful and empty. If this continues you will eventually become depressed and even reach breakdown.

As your stress increases you find yourself all too easily adopting the *negative* characteristics of your Eight stress point. However, this need not be an inevitable progression. You can, instead, get in touch with the *positive* side.

Eight: **(Stress Point)**
- You attempt to bully and take control of people.
- You become irascible, impatient and demanding.
- You target others for blame or criticism.
- You mistrust people's motives and becomes callous.

+ *You are more assertive in getting personal needs met.*
+ *You are more confident, minimizing the need for approval.*

When you are secure you are generally more in touch with

the higher side of your personality style. As a Two this allows you to get in touch with your own needs and to take care of yourself. If this involves saying 'no' to the requests or demands of others, you can do so without disguise. If it means letting others take care of your needs, you welcome it. The result is that, when you give, there will be no strings attached, because you are free of the compulsion to justify your worth by being the continual helper.

All of this feeds into the *positive* strengths of your Four security point. But, here too there can be some *negatives*. Dealing with the pluses and minuses helps us grow.

Four: (Security Point)

+ *You are willing to explore your inner emotional world.*
+ *You accept loneliness, hurt and other painful feelings.*
+ *Your creative side reveals another source of self-worth.*
+ *You begin to say 'no' and search for personal space.*

- You overplay the 'martyr' to the point of depression.
- You envy others and become self-absorbed.

HELPFUL COPING CUES

❏ I am loved for myself, not for my service.
❏ I have a right to say "No".
❏ I need to take care of myself first.
❏ I don't have to justify my feelings.
❏ Love lets go; possessiveness clings on.
❏ *Love your neighbour as yourself, (Mk 12:31)*

THREES

If you have adopted this personality style you are gifted in many ways. In particular, you are:

- [ ] adaptable
- [ ] outgoing
- [ ] industrious
- [ ] energetic
- [ ] efficient
- [ ] optimistic
- [ ] self-confident
- [ ] pragmatic
- [ ] goal-oriented

However, like everyone else, you have your flaws. For example, you can be:

- [ ] devious
- [ ] pretentious
- [ ] mendacious
- [ ] vain
- [ ] calculating
- [ ] narcissistic
- [ ] image-conscious
- [ ] manipulative
- [ ] callous

As an **Achiever** you are so competitive and image-conscious that you are prepared to deceive others in order to win or promote yourself. But you are so oblivious of your *deceit* that you deny how controlling and destructive it is.

SUBTYPES

Self-Preservation: *Focus on Security*
You equate being happy with being affluent and link your earning power to your personal security. A modest income is never enough. Therefore, financial health (a secure job, a good house and more than enough money), is a constant preoccupation.

As a workaholic, you 'do' lunch rather than eat it, and your focus is regularly on the next deal. You find it hard to relax and often bring your work home with you - even on vacations (which you rarely take). Afraid of being unemployed or made redundant, you develop work-related skills, invest as wisely as you can and seek to multiply your assets.

When all else fails you put on a show of being well-heeled and successful. This deception may not only fool others, but may also blind yourself to the reality of your situation.

Sexual: *Focus on Masculinity / Femininity*

You are a past master at looking attractive. You connect with others by looking good, radiating attention, appearing up-beat, cheerful and well-integrated - having your act together. You readily adapt to your partner's needs and style.

You go with whatever works in order to captivate and enthral. You especially work at being sexually pleasing. You dress well to suit the occasion, with an elegance even in your casual wear. If you are a woman you discreetly emphasize your femininity; if you are a man you are equally discreet in stressing your masculinity. Everything is done to impress your chosen partner.

Behind all the glamour, you are basically afraid that when people really get to know you, they will find there's nobody at home and will then reject you. Rather than risk this, you tend to move on to someone else.

Social: *Focus on Prestige*

Social status and club or committee membership are serious issues for you. Being the centre of attention wards off the anxiety attendant upon being anonymous. "You're just not anybody if nobody thinks you're somebody!" So you offer your services as president, secretary or treasurer, and court smart publicity, especially a photo in the paper or a radio or (better still) television interview.

As a public speaker your priority is to hold the audience's attention. You like being noticed and being looked up to. Playing a role and being a role-model are an accepted part of the prestige package. You dislike being upstaged by someone else. Indeed, you are hurt by it. You change your clothes with the role you are playing (theatregoer or cyclist), because it is essential to *look* the part.

WINGS 2 & 4

As you grew up you began to realize that your preening, self-promotion, and win-at-all-costs attitude were a turn-off. After all, most people prefer to come in contact with a real person who admits failures, rather than a performer continually hooked on success. So you began to rely on the personality style nearest to you to give your own style some balance. You may, for example, have spotted that *pretentiousness* is among the list of your characteristic flaws. But *authenticity* is one of the strengths of your Four Wing. When you learn to incorporate your wing-strength into your own personality style, you begin to soar.

Two Wing: When you access the strengths of your Two Wing you have a heart combination. The Two influence allows you to become more giving, especially if you're in a 'caring' profession. It also means that you will be more in touch with your heart and look for more intimacy in your life. Additionally, you will grow in your one-to-one relationship skills. There is a danger, though, that you will become even more outward-looking and blind to your deepest needs .

Four Wing: When you access the strengths of your Four Wing you have another heart combination, but this will help you in a different way. With it you learn to maintain a balance between your authentic self and the role you have adopted to play. You will be more willing to explore your own feelings and less likely to be satisfied with success at the expense of integrity. You will, however, need to be careful of becoming more 'precious', style-conscious and narcissistic.

Proper balance is achieved by accessing the strengths of *both* your wings and taking care to avoid their characteristic weaknesses. When you do so, you learn to let go of your obsessive Achiever viewpoint and begin to experience the advantages of other points of view.

ARROWS 9 & 6

The 'Arrow Theory' of the Enneagram can be very helpful when you are feeling either stressed or secure.

As an Achiever you are motivated by your need to succeed and be the centre of attention. You are stressed at the prospect of failure, loss of status or any threat to your ideal self-image.

Almost as soon as the pressure begins to build up, you gradually tend to slide to the lower end of your own personality style. When this happens your natural tendency is to 'rev up' the engine, diversify your interests, accept new tasks, press more flesh and generally move into overdrive in the fast lane. Your self-confidence may suffer and doubts about your abilities come to the surface. This may lead you to 'act out' and, chameleon-like, adopt an image to match the circumstances rather than reveal your true self.

As your stress increases you find yourself all too easily adopting the *negative* characteristics of your Nine stress point. However, this need not be an inevitable progression. You can, instead, get in touch with the *positive* side.

Nine: (Stress Point)
- You lose touch with your outer as well as inner self.
- You lose confidence and become less productive.
- You redouble your efforts but lose sight of your aims.
- You anaesthetize feelings with food, drink, drugs etc.

+ *You contemplatively begin to see the bigger picture.*
+ *You slow down and learn to relax.*

When you are secure you are generally more in touch with the higher side of your personality style. As a Three this allows you to become more honest with yourself. This will lead you to rediscover your deepest feelings and risk expressing them more. When you do, you will find you become less superficial, mechanical and even cold in relationships. This, in turn, will help you accept failure and learn from it. As you begin to reveal your real self and take time out to nourish your spirit, you will become free of the compulsion to justify your worth by being the continual achiever.

All of this feeds into the *positive* strengths of your Six security point. But, here too there can be some *negatives*. Dealing with the pluses and minuses helps us grow.

Six: (Security Point)

+ *You become more 'present' to people.*
+ *You value loyalty to family and friends.*
+ *You embrace the team spirit and moderate 'limelighting'.*
+ *You open up to feelings through reflection.*

- You feel more dependent on the approval of others.
- Your anxiety levels and fear of rejection increase.

HELPFUL COPING CUES

❏ Don't just *do* something, *stand* there!
❏ I am responsible for what I tame.
❏ Dim the headlights and reveal your self.
❏ I'm loved for myself, not for what I do.
❏ Slow down and listen to your feelings.
❏ *Be still and know that I am God. (Ps 46:10)*

FOURS

If you have adopted this personality style you are gifted in many ways. In particular, you are:

- [ ] intuitive
- [ ] expressive
- [ ] original

- [ ] creative
- [ ] cultured
- [ ] artistic

- [ ] sensitive
- [ ] stylish
- [ ] empathic

However, like everyone else, you have your flaws. For example, you can be:

- [ ] moody
- [ ] obstinate
- [ ] hyper-sensitive

- [ ] possessive
- [ ] critical
- [ ] depressive

- [ ] self-conscious
- [ ] spiteful
- [ ] masochistic

As an **Artist** you strive so hard for originality and uniqueness that you become envious of other people's gifts and abilities. But you are so oblivious of your *envy* that you deny how controlling and destructive it is.

SUBTYPES

Self-Preservation: *Focus on Risk*
You risk everything when it comes to feeling alive. There's a self-abandonment to your recklessness which is not too remote from an acceptance of death (suicide). Living on the edge is an adrenalin rush and brings with it a longed-for intensity of living, which makes normal routine living pale by comparison.

You can't stand playing it safe and being predictable. You regularly 'up the ante' on feeling alive (thrill-seeking, law-breaking, promiscuity, gambling etc.). By throwing caution to the winds, you succeed in transforming your inner pain into a meaningful energy which lifts you out of the ordinary. If the risk pays off (in terms of wealth, friend-ship or happiness) the cycle goes on, as you again dice with losing what you have gained. You relate to the saying: "Don't fence me in."

Sexual: *Focus on Competition*
You distract yourself from your need to be special and your feelings of loss by competing for attention. This is particularly so with colleagues or rivals, though not with close friends. Your powerful need for approval increases your energy levels, and you are determined to prove how desirable you are. Your competitiveness is generally self-referencing ("I'll show her *I'm* as good as he is.")

When successful, your self-worth is boosted. When you fail, your self-esteem is shattered and you change from being competitive to being a rival. This can range all the way from bad-mouthing and spitefulness, to an intense and vindictive hatred. Your compulsion to push your partner away in order to be able to win him/her back again, gives you the feeling of being in control, but is ultimately self-defeating.

Social: *Focus on Shame*
Since you never feel good enough or as talented as others, shame is your constant inner companion. You have low self-esteem and envy other people's achievements. This is a source of painful embarrassment to you in company. Shame is a product of questioning your own inner worth and results in feelings of inadequacy, failure, exclusion and unimportance.

You retreat into the shadows in case others discover how flawed you are and will then reject you. Your hyper-sensitivity to the slightest snub is in inverse proportion to your yearning to be acknowledged as special. You have a fear of being ignored or unwanted, especially at social gatherings. You rely on image or involvement to compensate (e.g. making strong dress statements, or seeking positions of authority or gold-circle club membership).

WINGS 3 & 5

As you grew up you began to realize that your mournful hangdog approach, as well as your roller-coaster moods and dramatic expression of feelings were a turn-off. After all, most people prefer to deal with the ordinary and everyday rather than the unique and highly sensitive. So you began to rely on the personality style nearest to you to give your own style some balance. You may, for example, have spotted that a clinging *possessiveness* is among the list of your characteristic flaws. But *detachment* is one of the strengths of your Five Wing. When you learn to incorporate your wing-strength into your own personality style, you begin to soar.

Three Wing: When you access the strengths of your Three Wing you have a heart combination. The Three influence allows you to deal with tasks more efficiently and to become more career orientated. The Three's practical, down-to-earth efficiency enables you to survive amid the humdrum and the everyday. Additionally, you begin to accept that you can have what you long for, provided you are prepared to work for it. There is a danger, though, that you will become even more self-centred and overidentify with the dramatic role you have chosen for yourself.

Five Wing: When you access the strengths of your Five Wing you have a heart/head combination, and this will help you in a different way. With it you learn to become more stable, because thinking moderates (even suppresses) feelings. You will also find it easier to remain detached and to analyse calmly what is happening to you. You will, however, need to be careful not to become more shy, retiring and aloof.

Proper balance is achieved by accessing the strengths of *both* your wings and taking care to avoid their characteristic weaknesses. When you do so, you learn to let go of

your obsessive Artist viewpoint and begin to experience the advantages of other points of view.

ARROWS 2 & 1

The 'Arrow Theory' of the Enneagram can be very helpful when you are feeling either stressed or secure.

As an Artist you are motivated by your need to be special and to be understood. You are stressed by misunderstanding, by vulgar insensitivity and by conflict in feelings and relationships.

Almost as soon as the pressure begins to build up, you gradually tend to slide to the lower end of your own personality style. When this happens your natural tendency is for your mood swings to increase. The intensity of your feelings churns you up so much that you frequently become sick and have to take to your bed. However, this or any other form of retiring (isolation) can make you feel even worse. You become quite vulnerable, begin to blame yourself, slip into a depressive state and even entertain thoughts of suicide to stop the pain.

As your stress increases you find yourself all too easily adopting the *negative* characteristics of your Two stress point. However, this need not be an inevitable progression. You can, instead, get in touch with the *positive* side.

Two: *(Stress Point)*
- You deny your own needs and concentrate on others.
- You attempt to 'buy' love to fill the aching loneliness.
- You latch on to another in a dependent role.
- You seek attention by developing unusual illnesses.

+ *You become more outgoing and less self-obsessed.*
+ *You relate more dispassionately with people.*

When you are secure you are generally more in touch with the higher side of your personality style. As a Four this allows you to appreciate how special you already are. You begin to realize that the extraordinary is only the ordinary unwrapped. Everyone is, therefore, unique, and ought to be celebrated rather than envied. The past and future no longer need to be given exaggerated importance, because the present is all there is. Living to the full in the 'now' relieves you of the burden of fretting or fantasizing about what has been or might be.

All of this feeds into the *positive* strengths of your One security point. But, here too there can be some *negatives*. Dealing with the pluses and minuses helps us grow.

One: *(Security Point)*
+   *You begin to live in the real world, flaws and all.*
+   *You gain more control over your feelings.*
+   *You concentrate on the positive rather than the negative.*
+   *You develop down-to-earth, practical everyday skills.*

-    You feel ashamed at not measuring up to standards.
-    You are critical and angry when things don't work out.

HELPFUL COPING CUES

❑ Bloom where you are planted!
❑ The extraordinary is the ordinary unwrapped.
❑ The mess is part of the reality.
❑ I am not my feelings; I can control them.
❑ I am a good and loving person.
❑ *Think of the flowers. (Lk 12:27)*

FIVES

If you have adopted this personality style you are gifted in many ways. In particular, you are:

- observant
- self-contained
- wise

- perceptive
- analytical
- objective

- reflective
- detached
- sensitive

However, like everyone else, you have your flaws. For example, you can be:

- withdrawn
- arrogant
- non-assertive

- cerebral
- superior
- unfeeling

- stingy
- remote
- uninvolved

As an **Observer** you strive so hard for meaningful information that, when you get it, you hoard it rather than part with it. But you are so oblivious of your *avarice* that you deny how controlling and destructive it is.

SUBTYPES

Self-Preservation: *Focus on Home*
You are basically an introvert and see your home as your castle. It may not be fortified or have a moat, wall or trees around it, but it really is a sanctuary for you when you close the front door and shut out the rest of the world. Dealing with people tends to drain you of energy, so you need this private familiar space to recuperate, reflect and think. Generally only close friends are ever invited in. You dislike intrusions (door-to-door salespeople, phone calls) and noise (traffic or neighbours).

You pare down your requirements and possessions to the basic minimum. You believe that life only gets complicated when people have more than they need. What you *do* have is therefore very important to you, and needs to be respected. You are stingy with time and money and you're self-reliant.

Sexual: *Focus on Trust / Confidence*

You share confidences and secrets with the people you trust. These confidences are etched in your memory and savoured in solitude. They can become very meaningful to you - the more so since such outpourings are so infrequent. Indeed, you positively tingle with power when you hold on to information and opt *not* to tell others what you know. Love and friendship are more likely to be expressed physically than spoken aloud. For you, touch is a more intimate symbol of trust than talk.

You protect your boundaries and maintain your privacy by keeping personal relationships separate from each other. Your avarice will not let you share openly. Prior consultation and agreement with you is vital before people dare to share your secrets with others. Though greedy for meaningful encounters and conversations, you generally don't initiate either.

Social: *Focus on Cultural Symbols*

You frequently appear more extroverted than the other Observer subtypes. Grasping the big picture boosts your confidence, so you seek to understand the underlying models and symbols in your field of interest. This enables you to access the deeper meaning and significance of events.

In an information age, knowledge of the key systems is power. Spreadsheet procedures, paradigm shifts, analytical surveys, pattern analysis and information models of all kinds allow you to be forewarned and so forearmed. This is your way of feeling safe and protected.

Totems, emblems, codes, hierarchies, cultural symbols, gurus and experts are important because they are able to impart wisdom on how things are organized and hang together in a coherent whole.

34

WINGS 4 & 6

As you grew up you began to realize that your aloofness and superiority, as well as your generally cerebral non-involvement in the sensual hurly-burly of life were a turn-off. After all, most people prefer to deal with flesh-and-blood characters who are open to the give-and-take of life. So you began to rely on the personality style nearest to you to give your own style some balance. You may, for example, have spotted that a *lack of feeling* is among the list of your characteristic flaws. But *feeling* is one of the strengths of your Four Wing. When you learn to incorporate your wing-strength into your own personality style, you begin to soar.

Four Wing: When you access the strengths of your Four Wing you have a head/heart combination. The Four influence allows you to get in touch with your feelings and emotions and begin to express them openly. You become more empathetic with people's problems. Additionally, your intellectual reserve is balanced by more artistic and creative drives. There is a danger, though, that you will become even more introspective and hyper-sensitive to the slights you experience.

Six Wing: When you access the strengths of your Six Wing you have a head combination, and this will help you in a different way. With it you learn to become more actively involved and dutiful without embarrassment. No longer a total loner, you experience the joys of belonging and being part of a group. You will, however, need to be careful not to become more self-questioning and lacking in confidence, because the Six energy can heighten your natural caution with doubts and fears.

Proper balance is achieved by accessing the strengths of *both* your wings and taking care to avoid their characteristic weaknesses. When you do so, you learn to let go of

your arrogant Observer viewpoint and begin to experience the advantages of other points of view.

ARROWS 7 & 8

The 'Arrow Theory' of the Enneagram can be very helpful when you are feeling either stressed or secure.

As an Observer you are motivated by your need to know and to understand. You are stressed when required to share your feelings or to get personally involved in the nuts-and-bolts of projects.

Almost as soon as the pressure begins to build you gradually tend to slide to the lower end of your own personality style. When this happens your natural tendency is to retreat to your ivory tower and pull up the ladder. You may grow even more remote and tend to say and do nothing. To ease the pain you may try to shut down your feelings, but all you really succeed in doing is become lonelier and more alienated.

As your stress increases you find yourself all too easily adopting the *negative* characteristics of your Seven stress point. However, this need not be an inevitable progression. You can, instead, get in touch with the *positive* side.

Seven: (Stress Point)
- You become distracted by all the 'head' stuff.
- You doubly avoid painful involvement.
- You withdraw even further from real life concerns.
- You lose focus by daydreaming and fantasizing.

+ *You blossom and become less shy and self-conscious.*
+ *You begin to enjoy new and adventurous experiences.*

When you are secure you are generally more in touch with the higher side of your personality style. As a Five this allows you to change your one-way-mirror for a pane of glass and become more open and trusting. You have a lot

36

to offer others when you dare to share. You begin to understand the mysterious dynamic of giving and receiving. When secure you are more willing to trust your instincts and listen to your heart. You become more involved in social justice issues, and are prepared to stand up and be counted. You begin to find a direct outlet for your anger and are even willing to face your fear of looking foolish in public.

All of this feeds into the *positive* strengths of your Eight security point. But, here too there can be some *negatives*. Dealing with the pluses and minuses helps us grow.

Eight: *(Security Point)*
+ *You get in touch with the body and the physical.*
+ *Your 'can-do' attitude leads to involvement in issues.*
+ *You feel energized and learn to trust gut instincts.*
+ *You speak out and become more pro-active.*

- You openly put people down with well-chosen words.
- You insensitively dismiss other people's feelings.

HELPFUL COPING CUES

❏ What goes around, comes around.
❏ The head doesn't have all the answers.
❏ Roll up your sleeves and get stuck in!
❏ I have feelings too.
❏ My body is vital to my well-being.
❏ *The Word became flesh and dwelt among us. (Jn 1:14)*

SIXES

If you have adopted this personality style you are gifted in many ways. In particular, you are:

☐ loyal   ☐ dutiful   ☐ hospitable
☐ caring   ☐ idealistic   ☐ prudent
☐ respectful   ☐ trustworthy   ☐ courageous

However, like everyone else, you have your flaws. For example, you can be:

☐ fearful   ☐ timid   ☐ suspicious
☐ indecisive   ☐ defensive   ☐ anxious
☐ authoritarian   ☐ aggressive   ☐ paranoid

As a **Supporter** you strive so hard to belong that you become fearful of not honouring your commitments. But you are so oblivious of your *fear* that you deny how controlling and destructive it is.

SUBTYPES

Self-Preservation: *Focus on Warmth*
You need constant reassurance that you are loved, and feel safest when you experience warmth and affection from friends and colleagues. You show love to get love. It pays off to be loyal to friends because then there is a good chance they will remain loyal in return. "One for all, and all for one." If there is a falling out, you make every effort to mend fences, even though you may still be annoyed or angry.

    Safe havens and security zones are vital to feeling protected. Belonging is crucial to you, since "no man is an island." Any coolness, aloofness or lack of communication makes you worry and doubt. You then parse and analyse to see what you might have done wrong. Your survival strategy is to redouble your efforts at friendship so as to disarm any threat to your safety.

Sexual: *Focus on Strength / Beauty*
Your doubting nature makes it hard for you to accept that others are sincere or friendly, even though you long for this. You are devastated by the prospect of betrayal and dislike the feelings of helplessness and dependence which accompany your reliance on others. You feel secure when you know others really care for you.

To conceal your fear, you put on a show of strength by trying to impress others with your tough logic and intimidating knowledge. Failing that, you may use sarcastic remarks or barbed wit to get others to back off. You may seek to strengthen your physique by working out, believing that by staying in shape you will be able to defend yourself better if need be. You also cultivate beauty, and feel secure when you are sexually attractive or seductively made up.

Social: *Focus on Duty*
You feel safe as part of a team and do not trust one-man-band operations. Worried about taking on extra responsibilities, you feel anxious when offered promotion. Since you fear criticism or embarrassment, you prefer to be in supporting roles rather than in the limelight.

You are reassured when you receive approval from team leaders. This minimizes your self-doubt. You also like to know where you stand and what is expected of you, otherwise you feel insecure and out on a limb. You are a conscientious rule-keeper and regularly refer things to authority figures, including those whose voices you carry around in your head. You give one-hundred-per-cent commitment to church, social, charity or self-help groups, and to deserving causes for the underprivileged.

WINGS 5 & 7

As you grew up you began to realize that your general fearfulness, your compliance and indecisiveness (phobic Six) or your aggression and risk-taking (counterphobic Six) were a turn-off. After all, most people prefer those who rely on their own inner authority and neither give it away nor hide their insecurities under a mask of appearing tough. So you began to rely on the personality style nearest to you to give your own style some balance. You may, for example, have spotted that *indecision* is among the list of your characteristic flaws. But *decisiveness* is one of the strengths of your Five Wing. When you learn to incorporate your wing-strength into your own personality style, you begin to soar.

Five Wing: When you access the strengths of your Five Wing you have a head combination. The Five influence allows you to become more observant, contemplative and private. You may also become more objective. Additionally, it can help you mitigate your workaholic tendencies by emphasizing both your perceptiveness and detachment. There is a danger, though, that you may become even more security conscious, more sceptical, and more fearful of getting in touch with your feelings.

Seven Wing: When you access the strengths of your Seven Wing you have another head combination, and this will help you in a different way. With it your natural fearfulness and inflexibility in thinking and acting will be balanced by spontaneity and an innovative spirit. This will allow you to network better and become more hospitable, fun-loving, convivial and sociable - all without worrying about neglecting your duties! You will, however, need to be careful lest you run even faster from your fears or take yourself less seriously.

Proper balance is achieved by accessing the strengths of

both your wings and taking care to avoid their characteristic weaknesses. When you do so, you learn to let go of your compulsive Supporter viewpoint and begin to experience the advantages of other points of view.

ARROWS 3 & 9

The 'Arrow Theory' of the Enneagram can be very helpful when you are feeling either stressed or secure.

As a Supporter you are motivated by your need for security and fear of making mistakes. You are stressed when uncertain, when in leadership roles and when you see the rules being broken.

Almost as soon as the pressure begins to build up, you gradually tend to slide to the lower end of your own personality style. When this happens your natural tendency is to become even more anxious than usual and to mistrust the adequacy of your inner resources. As your self-doubts increase you may become more wary, suspicious, and closed to other points of view. This may also bring out your rebellious streak.

As your stress increases you find yourself all too easily adopting the *negative* characteristics of your Three stress point. However, this need not be an inevitable progression. You can, instead, get in touch with the *positive* side.

Three: (Stress Point)
- You use work to blot out feelings of anxiety.
- You find security in a role, uniform or profession.
- You accept that the end justifies the means.
- You're unwilling to attempt the new for fear of failure.

+ *You focus on what's possible and take the initiative.*
+ *You disarm doubts with positive decision-making.*

When you are secure you are generally more in touch with the higher side of your personality style. As a Six this allows you to take charge of your choices and begin to trust your own inner authority. In effect it means that you become more independent and self-reliant. When this happens, you find that you become less riddled with doubts and far more proactive in dealing with problems. As your confidence increases, you are prepared to believe the best about people and not project deviance on to them. You also become creative when it comes to rules and regulations, recognizing that the spirit is more important than the letter of the law.

All of this feeds into the *positive* strengths of your Nine security point. But, here too there can be some *negatives*. Dealing with the pluses and minuses helps us grow.

Nine: *(Security Point)*
+ *You feel no need to be a permanent watchdog.*
+ *You relax into a non-competitive mode.*
+ *You become more supportive, warm and empathetic.*
+ *You gain a broader perspective through sitting back.*

- You become listless, uninterested and inactive.
- You deal with worries by anaesthetizing them.

HELPFUL COPING CUES

❑ Toot your own horn!
❑ Since I am loved, there's no reason to fear.
❑ Light a candle rather than curse the darkness.
❑ My authority comes from within.
❑ I have the courage of my own convictions.
❑ *I am with you, always. (Mt 28:20)*

SEVENS

If you have adopted this personality style you are gifted in many ways. In particular, you are:

- optimistic
- creative
- imaginative
- gregarious
- childlike
- resilient
- fun-loving
- joyful
- adventurous

However, like everyone else, you have your flaws. For example, you can be:

- escapist
- unreliable
- narcissistic
- distracted
- hedonistic
- addictive
- superficial
- undisciplined
- manic

As an **Optimist** you strive so hard to be happy and avoid pain that you become addicted to pleasure-seeking. But you are so oblivious of your *gluttony* that you deny how controlling and destructive it is.

SUBTYPES

Self-Preservation: *Focus on Family*
Like-minded friends are essential to you, and you value the support network these provide. You like having a solid home base and generally spend a lot of time there, or return regularly to catch up on the latest news and monitor the progress of a variety of projects. Sometimes it feels as if you have never been away, as you seem to be able to pick up things just where you left off. You dislike feeling that you have missed out on anything.

The plans you make with others for adventurous things to do are almost as enjoyable as the reality. A good plan will ensure that you experience as much as possible.

Variety and excitement are the spice of life and are provided by your 'family' network. You are prepared to take risks once the odds are in your favour. You tend to be calculating rather than reckless.

Sexual: *Focus on Fascination*
You are forever fascinated to discover new and exciting people and unusual or challenging things to do. You succeed in giving some people your exclusive and undivided attention, to such an extent that they are delightedly bowled over by the compliment. You get an immense kick from new one-to-one relationships, and effortlessly succeed in inserting yourself into other people's lives.

When the lustre begins to fade, you romanticize the relationship to increase its intensity and your own boredom threshold. However, your charm is so seductive that you can sometimes end up enmeshed and feeling trapped. You avoid commitment by continually moving on to another relationship which offers more interesting possibilities - often to the dismay of those you have originally captivated.

Social: *Focus on Sacrifice*
You are willing to delay gratification for a big enough reward, such as the well-being or happiness of the group. You appear more anxious, impatient and determined than other Optimist subtypes. This is often because the burden of being responsible for the group's welfare clashes with your not wanting to be tied down, and with your constant longing for fun and adventure.

You like positive people who can enjoy life. An enjoyment shared is an enjoyment doubled. Experiences are heightened in company, so you feel obliged to endure the seemingly endless time-wasting of the group decision-making process in order to experience the stimulation of being with interesting people. Other people's limitations frustrate you, but you nevertheless cultivate a large circle of friends.

WINGS 6 & 8

As you grew up you began to realize that your clowning around, your glibness, fantasizing, lack of follow-through and commitment were a turn-off. After all, most people prefer to be with rather more stable, responsible and realistic companions. So you began to rely on the personality style nearest to you to give your own style some balance. You may, for example, have spotted that *non-commitment* is among the list of your characteristic flaws. But *loyalty* is one of the strengths of your Six Wing. When you learn to incorporate your wing-strength into your own personality style, you begin to soar.

Six Wing: When you access the strengths of your Six Wing you have a head combination. The Six influence moderates your 'reckless-adventurer' streak with a sense of duty. It also helps you plan for problems as well as for joys. Additionally, you become more 'grounded' and present to people. There is a danger, though, that you may become more fearful and inclined to bravado in the face of what seems a hostile and threatening world.

Eight Wing: When you access the strengths of your Eight Wing you have a head/gut combination, and this will help you in a different way. With it, your natural happy-go-lucky approach is modified by added survival instincts. You develop a sense of realism in planning and moderation in pleasure-seeking. You become more direct and self-assertive and develop a greater tolerance for pain. You will, however, need to be careful lest you become even more driven in your compulsive consumption of people and things.

Proper balance is achieved by accessing the strengths of *both* your wings and taking care to avoid their characteristic weaknesses. When you do so, you learn to let go of your compulsive Optimist viewpoint and begin to experience the advantages of other points of view.

ARROWS 1 & 5

The 'Arrow Theory' of the Enneagram can be very helpful when you are feeling either stressed or secure.

As an Optimist you are motivated by your need to be happy and to avoid pain. You are stressed when tied down to a single project or forced to confront painful issues.

Almost as soon as the pressure begins to build up, you gradually tend to slide to the lower end of your own personality style. When this happens your natural tendency is to retreat into your head. You may start calculating, rationalizing and, above all, planning - anything to avoid having to actually *do* something. You may clown around, make jokes and pretend it's a big laugh. Or you may indulge in day-dreaming about the good times you experienced in the past or hope for in the future.

As your stress increases you find yourself all too easily adopting the *negative* characteristics of your One stress point. However, this need not be an inevitable progression. You can, instead, get in touch with the *positive* side.

One: (Stress Point)
- You become more judgemental and hypercritical.
- You develop 'either-or', 'black-and-white' thinking.
- You feel imprisoned and robbed of your natural zest.
- You feel resentful, peeved, dissatisfied and irritable.

+ *You keep your promises and meet your deadlines.*
+ *You delay gratification and put others first.*

When you are secure you are generally more in touch with the higher side of your personality style. As a Seven this allows you to become anchored in the present. You become willing to accept the rough with the smooth, and hold in balance life's mixture of joys and sorrows. You are prepared to commit yourself to people and projects in spite of the problems, and are ready to face the music rather than try to compose another tune. You no longer need to treat serious issues as a joke, attempting to laugh them off or explain them away.

All of this feeds into the *positive* strengths of your Five security point. But, here too there can be some *negatives*. Dealing with the pluses and minuses helps us grow.

Five: (Security Point)

+ *You look at things in depth rather than superficially.*
+ *You accept the importance of being quiet and contemplative.*
+ *You learn objectivity through being more reflective.*
+ *You are better able to make do with less consumables.*

- You avoid responsibilities by living in your head.
- You try to get a quick theoretical fix on people.

HELPFUL COPING CUES

❏ No seed ever sees the flower.

❏ Settle down and centre yourself.

❏ Happiness is an inside job.

❏ Less is more.

❏ Face the music and dance.

❏ *Your sorrow will turn to joy. (Jn 16:20)*

EIGHTS

If you have adopted this personality style you are gifted in many ways. In particular, you are:

- resourceful
- energetic
- just

- earthy
- direct
- powerful

- self-confident
- fearless
- passionate

However, like everyone else, you have your flaws. For example, you can be:

- aggressive
- possessive
- intimidating

- domineering
- confrontational
- vindictive

- insensitive
- controlling
- punitive

As a **Leader** you strive so hard to control and experience life to the full that your passion becomes overwhelming. But you are so oblivious of your *lust* that you deny how controlling and destructive it is.

SUBTYPES

Self-Preservation: *Focus on Survival*
You take all the necessary steps, no matter how risky, to make sure you will survive. If this means putting razor-wire on the walls, stocking up refrigerators with provisions, or checking out where to get at a wide variety of essential supplies with the least amount of effort, you will do so. You will not allow yourself to be deprived of the necessities of life.

Nor will you rely on others for your security. You are naturally independent and self-contained. You will do what it takes to protect your property, your loved ones and yourself. You feel safe when everything you need is within your grasp, when you can observe what's going on and can control events. You do not want to be beholden to anyone, and prefer not to borrow or to be in another's debt.

Sexual: *Focus on Possession / Surrender*
You are a passionate, high-energy, take-charge kind of person who must live life to the full and be in control of the situation. Your relationships are intense and generally with people who can stand their ground and hold their own in an argument. Indeed, arguments serve to bring you closer to your partners and friends, because you see 'fighting' as a way of getting at the truth and testing the mettle of the people you care about.

You need to feel central to people's lives, to be consulted on issues which involve you, and to have people open up to you when difficulties arise.

When your possessiveness is satisfied and your involvement in people's lives allows you to be sure of their loyalty, you can surrender control and allow yourself to become vulnerable and childlike.

Social: *Focus on Friendship*
What matters most to you is the loyalty of good friends. These will have been thoroughly tested for their honesty, integrity and calmness under fire. You know where you stand with such friends and stick by them, often at great personal cost. You are very protective of friends, but encourage them to become self-reliant like yourself. Your friendships can last a lifetime.

When there is real trust there is a freedom to be yourself, to let off steam and to allow feelings of vulnerability to surface.

Your stamina and zest for life are manifested in long and deep conversations and in your ability to party all night, expecting others to keep up with you. However, when mutual trust is betrayed, you cut people dead and may even seek to get your own back.

As you grew up you began to realize that your thick-skinned insensitivity, your belligerent behaviour and bullying approach were a turn-off. After all, most people prefer to be treated as equals rather than overwhelmed into submission. So you began to rely on the personality style nearest to you to give your own style some balance. You may, for example, have spotted that *intimidation* is among the list of your characteristic flaws. But *gentleness* is one of the strengths of your Nine Wing. When you learn to incorporate your wing-strength into your own personality style, you begin to soar.

Seven Wing: When you access the strengths of your Seven Wing you have a gut/head combination. The Seven influence allows you to get in touch with your inner child, to lighten up and become more relaxed and light-hearted with people. You become more creative and imaginative. Additionally, you are not as fiercely competitive or as prone to throw your weight around. There is a danger, though, that your appetite for food and consumables may become more voracious.

Nine Wing: When you access the strengths of your Nine Wing you have a gut combination, and this will help you in a different way. With it your natural passionate involvement in life is tempered by a laid-back self-forgetfulness. You are not as intense and learn to use your energy economically. You become more accepting of half-measures, more sensitive to other people's feelings and learn to 'go with the flow'. You will, however, need to be careful lest you rely too heavily on drink or other anaesthetizing agents, or become cynically dismissive of people's pain.

Proper balance is achieved by accessing the strengths of *both* your wings and taking care to avoid their characteristic weaknesses. When you do so, you learn to let go of

your compulsive Leader viewpoint and begin to experience the advantages of other points of view.

ARROWS 5 & 2

The 'Arrow Theory' of the Enneagram can be very helpful when you are feeling either stressed or secure.

As a Leader you are motivated by your need to be in control. You are stressed when faced with your own weakness or having to reveal your vulnerable inner child to others.

Almost as soon as the pressure begins to build up, you gradually tend to slide to the lower end of your own personality style. When this happens your natural tendency to excess is activated, so you may become more aggressive, ride roughshod over people and seek to manipulate and control situations even more blatantly. You believe that "when the going gets tough, the tough get going", and that you have to "do unto others *before* they do unto you".

As your stress increases you find yourself all too easily adopting the *negative* characteristics of your Five stress point. However, this need not be an inevitable progression. You can, instead, get in touch with the *positive* side.

Five: **(Stress Point)**
- You become less active and involved in life.
- You express your feelings less and less.
- You develop a 'loner' mentality.
- You arrogantly dismiss the feelings of others.

+ *You calm down and think before acting.*
+ *You distance your feelings and become more objective.*

When you are secure you are generally more in touch with the higher side of your personality style. As an Eight this encourages you to open up to others and let them see your own vulnerability without expecting them to take advantage of you when they see your weakness. You are prepared to accept help and acts of kindness without looking for the hidden strings attached. You empower others so that they can stand up for themselves, confident that they will not turn against you. You show consideration and respect for other people's rights rather than walk all over them.

All of this feeds into the *positive* strengths of your Two security point. But, here too there can be some *negatives*. Dealing with the pluses and minuses helps us grow.

Two: *(Security Point)*
+   *You are more accepting of the needs of others.*
+   *You learn to reveal your vulnerable 'inner child'.*
+   *You become more caring and less aggressive.*
+   *You appreciate the real strength of gentleness.*

-   You demand too much of others.
-   You react angrily when people are not appreciative.

HELPFUL COPING CUES

❏ A problem shared is a problem halved.
❏ Keep your powder dry!
❏ Honour and befriend your tender feelings.
❏ Others have feelings too.
❏ Cooperation is better than confrontation.
❏ *Here I am as one who serves. (Lk 22:27)*

NINES

If you have adopted this personality style you are gifted in many ways. In particular, you are:

- ☐ peaceful
- ☐ unpretentious
- ☐ gentle
- ☐ calm
- ☐ reassuring
- ☐ patient
- ☐ accommodating
- ☐ tolerant
- ☐ imperturbable

However, like everyone else, you have your flaws. For example, you can be:

- ☐ indolent
- ☐ apathetic
- ☐ obsessive
- ☐ forgetful
- ☐ oblivious
- ☐ addictive
- ☐ indecisive
- ☐ obstinate
- ☐ nihilistic

As a **Mediator** you strive so hard to avoid conflict that you become unassertive and self-forgetful. But you are so oblivious of your *sloth* that you deny how controlling and destructive it is.

SUBTYPES

Self-Preservation: *Focus on Appetite*
You protect yourself from the demands and vicissitudes of life by seeking to shut them out or ignore them altogether. So you may neglect what is important and replace it with the trivial.

Having made sure you are well supplied with provisions, you can binge on comfort eating and drinking, zonk out in front of the television or video, listen to the radio or your tape collection, and generally indulge in numbing behaviour to block out the pain or hassle.

When you dull your senses with these routine patterns of behaviour you don't have to act. This means you don't have to merge with others and so risk losing your own identity. Nor do you have to make a decision or take a stand and so risk experiencing isolation and separation from others.

Sexual: *Focus on Union*
You long for the wholeness which union with a special other brings. This other can be a lover, guru, leader, media personality, nature or God. You need union to give yourself focus and direction in life, and to provide a reason for being. When you are united with another, you feel as if you count for something and can no longer be ignored. Your desire for spiritual union can be very strong.

You want to merge with another, even at the risk of losing your own individuality. Caught up in the other, you think you have found yourself at last, yet are generally unaware of what is going on in your life. Your energy comes from that special other. You are happy when your partner is happy, and sad when you have no one with whom to merge.

Social: *Focus on Participation*
You like joining groups and attending meetings because you like the feeling of belonging, of being included and of being energized. However, you generally do not fully commit yourself to any group because of the possible conflicts. You are happiest remaining in the background, and often you are in two minds as to whether you want to belong or not.

Harmony within the group is important to you and you can work hard at achieving it. Ideally you want everybody to join in and to get along as one happy family. The group mentality reinforces your tendency to hide from yourself, while the energy you expend in group activities leaves little left over for you to use on your own inner work. You are content to lose yourself in the group and become all things to all people.

WINGS 8 & 1

As you grew up you began to realize that your general lack of focus, indecisiveness, tardiness and passive aggression were a turn-off. After all, most people prefer to be with those who bring zest, vitality and a certain amount of passion to life. So you began to rely on the personality style nearest to you to give your own style some balance. You may, for example, have spotted that *indolence* is among the list of your characteristic flaws. But *diligence* is one of the strengths of your One Wing. When you learn to incorporate your wing-strength into your own personality style, you begin to soar.

Eight Wing: When you access the strengths of your Eight Wing you have a gut combination. The Eight influence puts you more in touch with your own anger, so that instead of swallowing it and becoming passive-aggressive, you can learn a more direct way of expressing it. In doing so you also become less self-effacing. Additionally, you learn to deal with situations better by letting go of trivialities and concentrating on the essentials. There is a danger, though, that you may become even more stubborn and unmovable.

One Wing: When you access the strengths of your One Wing you have another gut combination, and this will help you in a different way. With it you begin to prioritize better, become energetic (though without overdoing it), and are more likely to face up to, rather than dodge, serious issues. You also become much more responsible and precise. You will, however, need to be careful lest you become so resentful that you become 'picky', self-critical and judgemental.

Proper balance is achieved by accessing the strengths of *both* your wings and taking care to avoid their characteristic weaknesses. When you do so, you learn to let go of

your compulsive Mediator viewpoint and begin to experience the advantages of other points of view.

ARROWS 6 & 3

The 'Arrow Theory' of the Enneagram can be very helpful when you are feeling either stressed or secure.

As a Mediator you are motivated by your need to be calm and at peace. You are stressed when you have to face difficult issues, meet deadlines or confront others.

Almost as soon as the pressure begins to build you gradually tend to slide to the lower end of your own personality style. When this happens your natural tendency is to shut down. This may involve a variety of tactics from leaving the room, going home to mother, not paying attention, concentrating on unimportant projects, falling asleep or numbing yourself out with alcohol. Another favourite ploy is to procrastinate. However, putting things on the long finger only delays the inevitable.

As your stress increases you find yourself all too easily adopting the *negative* characteristics of your Six stress point. However, this need not be an inevitable progression. You can, instead, get in touch with the *positive* side.

Six: (Stress Point)
- You see practically everything as a source of anxiety.
- You endlessly delay decision-making.
- Your poor self-image is magnified by increased doubts.
- You become locked into passivity and inertia.

+ *You develop practical lifeskills for supporting others.*
+ *You courageously begin to face up to problems.*

When you are secure you are generally more in touch with the higher side of your personality style. As a Nine this allows you to become more focused and to wake up to the reality of your situation. When not entranced, you are better able to get in touch with what you feel and are more likely to be forthright and direct in demanding that your legitimate needs be met. You no longer neglect yourself or take yourself for granted, but take better care of your health and general appearance. Effectively, you are more energetic and better able to act on your own behalf and on behalf of others. This means you no longer have to use substitute strategies or avoiding tactics to get what you want.

All of this feeds into the *positive* strengths of your Three security point. But, here too there can be some *negatives*. Dealing with the pluses and minuses helps us grow.

Three: (Security Point)

+ *You get the 'kick-start' you need to get on with life.*
+ *You become more positive about your self-image.*
+ *You focus your attention on what needs to be done.*
+ *You are energized by making confident choices.*

- You avoid facing your inner emotional life.
- You overburden yourself with too many projects.

HELPFUL COPING CUES

❏ Every journey begins with the first step.

❏ Face the problems - they won't go away.

❏ A stitch in time saves a Nine!

❏ I, too, am worthwhile and much loved.

❏ The truth is *in* there!

❏ *Every hair on your head is counted. (Lk 12:7)*

ABOUT THE AUTHORS

The authors are experienced presenters of Enneagram and Stress Management workshops which they have given to a wide range of business, educational and religious groups in several countries. They are also the authors of:

An Enneagram Guide: A Spirituality of Love in Brokenness
Stress and How to Deal With It
The Enneagram: The Quest for Self-Transcendence
Enneagram 2: A Spirituality of Brokenness

Éilís Bergin PBVM , is a member of the Presentation Congregation. Her ministries have included teaching, administration, workshops on Stress Management and Enneagram, and work with emotionally deprived children.

Eddie Fitzgerald SDB, was a member of the Salesians of Don Bosco. His ministries included teaching theology, media education, retreat giving, human development courses and television broadcasting. He was editor of *The Salesian Bulletin* for 23 years and director of SDB MEDIA. Fr Eddie's last book, *Cancer Busters,* was published one month before he died on 23 December 1999.

SDB MEDIA, Salesian College, Celbridge, Co. Kildare
Tel: (01) 627 5060
Fax: (01) 630 3601
E-mail: sdbmedia@eircom.net
Web: http://homepage.eircom.net/~sdbmedia